The Urantia Book

Foreword

0:0.1 (1.1) IN THE MINDS of the mortals of Urantia—that being the name of your world—there exists great confusion respecting the meaning of such terms as God, divinity, and deity.

The concept of God, divinity, and deity can be confusing for many people on Earth, also known as Urantia. These terms often refer to a supreme being or beings that are believed to have created and/or oversee the universe and everything in it. However, the specific nature and attributes of this supreme being or beings vary greatly depending on the religious or spiritual beliefs of the individual or culture. For some, God is a single, all-powerful entity that is omnipotent, omniscient, and omnipresent. For others, divinity may be seen as a collection of multiple gods or goddesses with specific domains or areas of influence. Still, others may not believe in a traditional concept of deity at all, and may instead see the universe as a natural, self-sustaining entity without any need for a divine creator. Ultimately, the meaning of these terms is highly subjective and can vary greatly among individuals and cultures.

Human beings are still more confused and uncertain about the relationships of the divine personalities designated by these numerous appellations.

The relationships between the various divine personalities referred to by terms like God, divinity, and deity are often a source of confusion and uncertainty for many people. This is because these terms can be used to refer to a wide range of different beings and concepts, and the specific nature and relationships of these divine personalities can vary greatly depending on the religious or spiritual beliefs of the individual or culture. For example, in some belief systems, God is seen as a single, all-powerful entity that is the creator and ruler of the universe, while other deities may be seen as lesser beings with specific areas of influence or power. In other belief systems, there may be multiple gods and goddesses who are seen as equals, or who are part of a hierarchy with a supreme being at the top. Additionally, some people may not believe in any divine beings at all, and may see the universe as a natural, self-sustaining entity without the need for a divine creator. Because of these many different beliefs and interpretations, it is not surprising that there is confusion and uncertainty about the relationships between these divine personalities.

Because of this conceptual poverty associated with so much ideational confusion, I have been directed to formulate this introductory statement in explanation of the meanings which should be attached to certain word symbols as they may be hereinafter used in those papers which the Orvonton corps of truth revealers have been authorized to translate into the English language of Urantia.

0:0.2 (1.2) It is exceedingly difficult to present enlarged concepts and advanced truth, in our endeavor to expand cosmic consciousness and enhance spiritual perception, when we are restricted to the use of a circumscribed language of the realm.

It can be challenging to effectively convey complex or advanced ideas and truths when using the limited language and vocabulary of a particular realm or domain. This is because language is a fundamental tool for communication and understanding, and the words and phrases we use to describe concepts are often deeply tied to the way we think and perceive the world around us. As a result, when trying to expand cosmic consciousness or enhance spiritual perception, it can be difficult to find the right words and phrases to accurately and effectively convey the ideas and truths being presented. This is especially true when the language being used is limited or circumscribed in some way, making it difficult to find the right words and phrases to accurately convey the intended meaning. In such cases, it may be necessary to use creative and imaginative language, or to draw on other forms of communication such as storytelling or visualization, in order to effectively convey the intended ideas and truths.

But our mandate admonishes us to make every effort to convey our meanings by using the word symbols of the English tongue. We have been instructed to introduce new terms only when the concept to be portrayed finds no terminology in English which can be employed to convey such a new concept partially or even with more or less distortion of meaning.

In this situation, the speaker or writer has been given a mandate, or a specific instruction, to make every effort to use the word symbols of the English language when conveying their meanings. This means that they are being asked to use the existing vocabulary and terminology of the English language to the greatest extent possible, rather than introducing new terms or phrases. The reason for this is that new terms can often be confusing or misleading, especially if they do not have an established meaning or if they are used to convey a concept that is not easily expressible using the existing language. As a result, the speaker or writer is being asked to only introduce new terms when there is no existing terminology in English that can be used to convey the concept without significant distortion of meaning. In other words, they are being asked to use the existing language as much as possible, and only introduce new terms when it is absolutely necessary in order to accurately convey the intended meaning.

0:0.3 (1.3) In the hope of facilitating comprehension and of preventing confusion on the part of every mortal who may peruse these papers, we deem it wise to present in this initial statement an outline of the meanings to be attached to numerous English words which are to be employed in designation of Deity and certain associated concepts of the things, meanings, and values of universal reality.

The speaker or writer of this text is trying to help readers understand and make sense of the ideas and concepts that will be presented in the papers they are writing. To do this, they have decided to provide an outline of the meanings that will be attached to various English words that will be used to refer to deity and other important concepts. The reason for doing this is to prevent confusion on the part of readers, and to make sure that everyone who reads the papers has a clear understanding of the words and phrases that will be used. By providing this outline, the speaker or writer is hoping to facilitate comprehension and ensure that readers are able to accurately interpret the ideas and concepts that are being presented. This will help to make the papers more accessible and understandable, and will help readers to engage with the ideas and concepts in a meaningful way.

0:0.4 (1.4) But in order to formulate this Foreword of definitions and limitations of terminology, it is necessary to anticipate the usage of these terms in the subsequent presentations. This Foreword is not, therefore, a finished statement within itself; it is only a definitive guide designed to assist those who shall read the accompanying papers dealing with Deity and the universe of universes which have been formulated by an Orvonton commission sent to Urantia for this purpose.

0:0.5 (1.5) Your world, Urantia, is one of many similar

inhabited planets which comprise the local universe of *Nebadon.* This universe, together with similar creations, makes up the superuniverse of *Orvonton,* from whose capital, Uversa, our commission hails. Orvonton is one of the seven evolutionary superuniverses of time and space which circle the never-beginning, never-ending creation of divine perfection—the central universe of *Havona.* At the heart of this eternal and central universe is the stationary Isle of Paradise, the geographic center of infinity and the dwelling place of the eternal God.

The text describes the hierarchical structure of the universe in which the planet Urantia, also known as Earth, is located. Urantia is said to be one of many inhabited planets that make up the local universe of Nebadon. This local universe, along with other similar creations, is part of the larger superuniverse of Orvonton. Orvonton is one of seven superuniverses that are part of an even larger creation known as the central universe of Havona. The central universe of Havona is said to be the never-beginning, never-ending creation of divine perfection, and at its heart is the stationary Isle of Paradise, which is the geographic center of infinity and the dwelling place of the eternal God. This hierarchical structure suggests that the universe is made up of many different levels, each with its own unique characteristics and functions, and that the planet Urantia is just one small part of this vast and complex cosmic structure.

0:0.6 (1.6) The seven evolving superuniverses in association with the central and divine universe, we commonly refer to as the *grand universe;* these are the now organized and inhabited creations. They are all a part of the *master universe,* which also embraces the uninhabited but mobilizing universes of outer space.

The text describes the concept of the grand universe, which is a term used to refer to the seven evolving superuniverses that are currently organized and inhabited, along with the central and divine universe of Havona. The grand universe is said to be part of the larger master universe, which also includes uninhabited but mobilizing universes of outer space. This suggests that the universe is composed of many different levels or realms, each with its own unique characteristics and functions. The grand universe is made up of the seven superuniverses that are currently inhabited and evolving, as well as the central and divine universe of Havona, which is eternal and unchanging. The master universe, on the other hand, includes not only the grand universe, but also other universes that are currently uninhabited but may be inhabited in the future. This hierarchy of universes highlights the vastness and complexity of the cosmic structure, and suggests that there is much more to the universe than what we can currently observe and understand.

I. Deity and Divinity

0:1.1 (2.1) The universe of universes presents phenomena of deity activities on diverse levels of cosmic realities, mind meanings, and spirit values, but all of these ministrations—personal or otherwise—are divinely co-ordinated.

The text is describing the universe of universes, which is a term used to refer to the entirety of the cosmic structure, including all of the inhabited and uninhabited universes, superuniverses, and other realms. The universe of universes is said to present phenomena of deity activities on diverse levels of cosmic realities, mind meanings, and spirit values. This suggests that there are many different levels or realms within the universe of universes, each with its own unique characteristics and functions, and that the divine beings known as deities are active on these different levels. However, despite the diversity of these levels and realms, the text suggests that all of the activities of the deities are divinely coordinated. This means that there is some sort of overarching plan or purpose that guides the actions of the deities, ensuring that they work together in harmony and support each other's efforts. This coordination among the deities helps to maintain the order and balance of the universe of universes, and allows for the continued evolution and growth of all the different levels and realms within it.

0:1.2 (2.2) DEITY is personalizable as God, is prepersonal and superpersonal in ways not altogether comprehensible by man. Deity is characterized by the quality of unity—actual or potential—on all supermaterial levels of reality; and this unifying quality is best comprehended by creatures as divinity.

The text is discussing the concept of deity, which is often used to refer to divine beings or supreme beings that are believed to have created and/or oversee the universe and everything in it. The text suggests that deity can be personalizable as God, meaning that it can take on a personal form or aspect that is understandable and relatable to human beings. At the same time, the text suggests that deity is also prepersonal and superpersonal in ways that are not entirely comprehensible by humans. This means that there are aspects of deity that are beyond the scope of human understanding and experience, and that cannot be easily explained or described using human language and concepts.

The text also suggests that deity is characterized by the quality of unity, which means that it has the ability to bring together different things or concepts into a single, cohesive whole. This unity can exist on all levels of reality, including those that are beyond the material realm and are therefore not accessible to human senses. The text suggests that this unifying quality of deity is best understood by creatures as divinity, and that it is this quality that makes deity unique and distinct from other things or concepts. In this way, the text is highlighting the complexity and mystery of deity, and the many different ways in which it can be understood and experienced.

0:1.3 (2.3) Deity functions on personal, prepersonal, and superpersonal levels. Total Deity is functional on the following seven levels:

0:1.4 (2.4) 1. *Static*—self-contained and self-existent Deity.

0:1.5 (2.5) 2. *Potential*—self-willed and self-purposive Deity.

0:1.6 (2.6) 3. *Associative*—self-personalized and divinely fraternal Deity.

0:1.7 (2.7) 4. *Creative*—self-distributive and divinely revealed Deity.

0:1.8 (2.8) 5. *Evolutional*—self-expansive and creature-identified Deity.

0:1.9 (2.9) 6. *Supreme*—self-experiential and creature-Creator-unifying Deity. Deity functioning on the first creature-identificational level as time-space overcontrollers of the grand universe, sometimes designated the Supremacy of Deity.

0:1.10 (2.10) 7. *Ultimate*—self-projected and time-space-transcending Deity. Deity omnipotent, omniscient, and omnipresent. Deity functioning on the second level of unifying divinity expression as effective overcontrollers and absonite upholders of the master universe. As compared with the ministry of the Deities to the grand universe, this absonite function in the master universe is tantamount to universal overcontrol and supersustenance, sometimes called the Ultimacy of Deity.

The text is discussing the different levels or modes of functioning of deity, which is a term used to refer to divine beings or supreme beings that are believed to have created and/or oversee the universe and everything in it. The text suggests that deity functions on personal, prepersonal, and superpersonal levels, and that total deity is functional on seven different levels. These levels are described as follows:

1. *Static – This level of deity is self-contained and self-existent, meaning that it does not depend on anything else for its existence or identity.*
2. *Potential – This level of deity is self-willed and self-purposive, meaning that it has the ability to make its own decisions and choices based on its own goals and*

objectives.

3. *Associative – This level of deity is self-personalized and divinely fraternal, meaning that it has the ability to take on a personal form or aspect, and that it is connected to other divine beings in a way that is similar to familial relationships.*
4. *Creative – This level of deity is self-distributive and divinely revealed, meaning that it has the ability to create and bring forth new things, and that it is able to reveal itself and its nature to others in a way that is accessible and understandable.*
5. *Evolutional – This level of deity is self-expansive and creature-identified, meaning that it has the ability to grow and change, and that it is able to identify with and understand the needs and experiences of creatures.*
6. *Supreme – This level of deity is self-experiential and creature-Creator-unifying, meaning that it is able to directly experience and understand the universe and everything in it, and that it has the ability to bring together creatures and the Creator into a single, unified whole.*
7. *Ultimate – This level of deity is self-projected and time-space-transcending, meaning that it is able to extend itself beyond the limitations of time and space, and that it has the ability to project itself into other realms and dimensions.*

Overall, the text suggests that deity has many different levels of functioning, each of which has its own unique characteristics and abilities. These levels of functioning allow deity to fulfill a wide range of roles and functions within the universe, and to interact with and support the evolution and growth of all the different levels and realms within it.

0:1.11 (2.11) *The finite level* of reality is characterized by creature life and time-space limitations. Finite realities may not have endings, but they always have beginnings—they are created. The Deity level of Supremacy may be conceived as a function in relation to finite existences.

The text is discussing the concept of finite reality, which is a term used to refer to the levels of reality that are characterized by creature life and time-space limitations.

Finite realities are distinguished from other levels of reality by the fact that they have beginnings, but may not have endings. This means that finite realities are created or brought into being by some external force or agency, but that they do not necessarily have an end or a final state. The text suggests that the level of reality known as the Deity level of Supremacy may be conceived as a function in relation to finite existences. This means that the Deity level of Supremacy is something that exists in relation to finite realities, and that it has a specific role or purpose in relation to these realities. This could imply that the Deity level of Supremacy has the ability to influence or shape the development and evolution of finite realities in some way, perhaps by providing guidance or support to the creatures that live within these realities. Overall, the text is highlighting the complex and hierarchical nature of the universe, and the many different levels and realms that make up its structure.

0:1.12 (2.12) *The absonite level* of reality is characterized by things and beings without beginnings or endings and by the transcendence of time and space. Absoniters are not created; they are eventuated—they simply are. The Deity level of Ultimacy connotes a function in relation to absonite realities. No matter in what part of the master universe, whenever time and space are transcended, such an absonite phenomenon is an act of the Ultimacy of Deity.

The text is discussing the concept of absonite reality, which is a term used to refer to levels of reality that are characterized by things and beings that do not have beginnings or endings, and that are able to transcend time and space. Absonite realities are distinguished from other levels of reality by the fact that the things and beings that exist within them are not created or brought into being by some external force or agency. Instead, they are said to be eventuated, which means that they simply are, without the need for a beginning or an end. The text suggests that the level of reality known as the Deity level of Ultimacy connotes a function in relation to absonite realities. This means that the Deity level of Ultimacy exists in relation to absonite realities, and that it has a specific role or purpose in relation to these realities. The text also suggests that whenever time and space are transcended, such an absonite phenomenon is an act of the Ultimacy of Deity. This implies that the Ultimacy of Deity has the ability to influence or shape the development and evolution of absonite realities in some way, and that it is responsible for the transcendence of time and space within these realities. Overall, the text is highlighting the complex and hierarchical nature of the universe, and the many different levels and realms that make up its structure.

0:1.13 (2.13) *The absolute level* is beginningless, endless, timeless, and spaceless. For example: On Paradise, time and space are nonexistent; the time-space status of Paradise is absolute. This level is Trinity attained, existentially, by the Paradise Deities, but this third level of unifying Deity expression is not fully unified experientially. Whenever, wherever, and however the absolute level of Deity functions, Paradise-absolute values and meanings are manifest.

The text is discussing the concept of the absolute level, which is a term used to refer to a level of reality that is beginningless, endless, timeless, and spaceless. The text gives the example of Paradise, which is said to be a realm or realm of existence that is characterized by the absence of time and space. This means that time and space do not exist on Paradise in the same way that they do on other levels of reality, and that the time-space status of Paradise is absolute. The text also suggests that the absolute level is Trinity attained, meaning that it is a level of existence that is characterized by the presence of the three persons of the Trinity – the Father, the Son, and the Holy Spirit – in a way that is existential, or real and actual. However, the text also suggests that this third level of unifying Deity expression is not fully unified experientially, meaning that the three persons of the Trinity are not fully united or integrated in their experiences or perceptions.

Overall, the text is suggesting that the absolute level is a realm or level of reality that is characterized by the absence of time and space, and by the presence of the three persons of the Trinity in a way that is existential. This level of reality is said to be manifest whenever, wherever, and however the absolute level of Deity functions, and it is associated with Paradise-absolute values and meanings. This suggests that the absolute level is a realm or level of existence that is of great significance and importance, and that it is closely associated with the ultimate goals and purposes of the divine beings known as deities.

0:1.14 (3.1) Deity may be existential, as in the Eternal Son; experiential, as in the Supreme Being; associative, as in God the Sevenfold; undivided, as in the Paradise Trinity.

The text is discussing the concept of deity, which is often used to refer to divine beings or supreme beings that are believed to have created and/or oversee the universe and everything in it. The text suggests that deity may take on different forms or aspects, depending on the context and the level of reality in which it is functioning. For example, the text suggests that deity may be existential, as in the case of the Eternal Son, which is one of the three persons of the Trinity. The text also suggests that deity may be experiential, as in the case of the Supreme Being, which is a term used to refer to a divine being that has the ability to directly experience and understand the universe and everything in it.

The text also suggests that deity may be associative, as in the case of God the Sevenfold, which is a term used to refer to the collective group of seven divine beings that are said to be responsible for the creation and governance of the universe. Finally, the text suggests that deity may be undivided, as in the case of the Paradise Trinity, which is a term used to refer to the three persons of the Trinity – the Father, the Son, and the Holy Spirit – when they are united or integrated in their nature, purpose, and experience.

Overall, the text is highlighting the complexity and diversity of deity, and the many different forms or aspects that it may take on depending on the context and the level of reality in which it is functioning. This suggests that deity is a multifaceted and mysterious concept, and that it is difficult to fully understand or explain using human language and concepts.

0:1.15 (3.2) Deity is the source of all that which is divine. Deity is characteristically and invariably divine, but all that which is divine is not necessarily Deity, though it will be co-ordinated with Deity and will tend towards some phase of unity with Deity—spiritual, mindal, or personal.

The text is discussing the concept of deity, which is often used to refer to divine beings or supreme beings that are believed to have created and/or oversee the universe and everything in it. The text suggests that deity is the source of all that which is divine, meaning that everything that has divine characteristics or attributes can be traced back to deity as its origin or source. The text also suggests that deity is characteristically and invariably divine, meaning that it has all of the characteristics and attributes that are typically associated with divinity, and that it is always divine in nature.

However, the text also suggests that not everything that is divine is necessarily deity, meaning that there are things or beings that have divine characteristics or attributes, but that are not deity themselves. The text suggests that these things or beings that are divine, but not deity, will be coordinated with deity and will tend towards some phase of unity with deity. This suggests that there is a close relationship between deity and all that which is divine, and that there is a tendency for things that are divine to become more closely aligned or united with deity over time. The text suggests that this unity may be spiritual, mindal, or personal in nature, depending on the specific context and the level of reality in which it occurs. Overall, the text is highlighting the central and important role of deity in the universe, and the many different ways in which it interacts with and influences other divine things and beings.

0:1.16 (3.3) DIVINITY is the characteristic, unifying, and co-ordinating quality of Deity.

0:1.17 (3.4) Divinity is creature comprehensible as truth, beauty, and goodness; correlated in personality as love, mercy, and ministry; disclosed on impersonal levels as justice, power, and sovereignty.

0:1.18 (3.5) Divinity may be perfect—complete—as on existential and creator levels of Paradise perfection; it may be imperfect, as on experiential and creature levels of time-space evolution; or it may be relative, neither perfect nor imperfect, as on certain Havona levels of existential-experiential relationships.

The text is discussing the concept of divinity, which is often used to refer to the characteristic, unifying, and co-ordinating quality of deity. The text suggests that divinity is something that is creature comprehensible, meaning that it can be understood and appreciated by creatures, or beings that exist within the universe. The text suggests that divinity is often understood in terms of three core concepts – truth, beauty, and goodness – which are closely related and intertwined.

The text also suggests that divinity may be correlated in personality, meaning that it may take on specific forms or aspects that are associated with personality. In particular, the text suggests that divinity may be correlated with three specific qualities – love, mercy, and ministry – which are often associated with personality, and which are believed to be essential for the proper functioning and development of creatures. The text also suggests that divinity may be disclosed on impersonal levels, meaning that it may be revealed or made known in ways that are not necessarily associated with personal beings or entities. In particular, the text suggests that divinity may be disclosed in terms of three specific qualities – justice, power, and sovereignty – which are often associated with impersonal levels of reality, and which are believed to be essential for the proper functioning and governance of the universe.

Overall, the text is suggesting that divinity is a complex and multifaceted concept, and that it has many different forms and aspects, depending on the specific context and the level of reality in which it is encountered. The text also suggests that divinity may be perfect, imperfect, or relative in nature, depending on the specific level of reality in which it is encountered, and that it has the ability to unify and co-ordinate the various levels and realms of the universe.

0:1.19 (3.6) When we attempt to conceive of perfection in all phases and forms of relativity, we encounter seven conceivable types:

0:1.20 (3.7) 1. Absolute perfection in all aspects.

0:1.21 (3.8) 2. Absolute perfection in some phases and

relative perfection in all other aspects.

0:1.22 (3.9) 3. Absolute, relative, and imperfect aspects in varied association.

0:1.23 (3.10) 4. Absolute perfection in some respects, imperfection in all others.

0:1.24 (3.11) 5. Absolute perfection in no direction, relative perfection in all manifestations.

0:1.25 (3.12) 6. Absolute perfection in no phase, relative in some, imperfect in others.

0:1.26 (3.13) 7. Absolute perfection in no attribute, imperfection in all.

The text is discussing the concept of perfection, and the various forms and types that it may take on when it is considered in relation to relativity. The text suggests that there are seven conceivable types of perfection that can be identified when considering perfection in all phases and forms of relativity. These seven types of perfection are as follows:

1. *Absolute perfection in all aspects – this type of perfection refers to a state or condition in which all aspects of something are absolutely perfect, with no imperfections or flaws of any kind.*
2. *Absolute perfection in some phases and relative perfection in all other aspects – this type of perfection refers to a state or condition in which some aspects of something are absolutely perfect, while other aspects are relatively perfect, meaning that they are perfect in relation to a specific context or set of circumstances.*
3. *Absolute, relative, and imperfect aspects in varied association – this type of perfection refers to a state or condition in which there are a mix of absolute, relative, and imperfect aspects, with no clear or consistent pattern or relationship between them.*
4. *Absolute perfection in some respects, imperfection in all others – this type of perfection refers to a state or condition in which some aspects of something are absolutely perfect, while all other aspects are imperfect.*
5. *Absolute perfection in no direction, relative perfection in all manifestations – this type of perfection refers to a state or*

condition in which there is no absolute perfection in any direction or aspect, but there is relative perfection in all manifestations, meaning that all aspects are perfect in relation to a specific context or set of circumstances.

6. *Absolute perfection in no phase, relative in some, imperfect in others – this type of perfection refers to a state or condition in which there is no absolute perfection in any phase or aspect, but there is relative perfection in some phases, and imperfection in others.*

7. *Absolute perfection in no attribute, imperfection in all – this type of perfection refers to a state or condition in which there is no absolute perfection in any attribute or characteristic, and all aspects are imperfect in some way.*

Overall, the text is suggesting that perfection is a complex and multifaceted concept, and that it can take on many different forms and types depending on the specific context and the level of relativity that is involved. The text is highlighting the various types of perfection that can be identified when considering perfection in relation to relativity, and is suggesting that there are many different ways in which perfection can be understood and interpreted.

II. God

0:2.1 (3.14) Evolving mortal creatures experience an irresistible urge to symbolize their finite concepts of God. Man's consciousness of moral duty and his spiritual idealism represent a value level—an experiential reality—which is difficult of symbolization.

The text is discussing the concept of God, and the ways in which mortal creatures (i.e. human beings) attempt to symbolize or represent their finite concepts of God using various symbols and images. The text suggests that there is an irresistible urge or impulse among mortal creatures to symbolize their concepts of God, which is driven by their consciousness of moral duty and their spiritual idealism. This suggests that human beings have a deep-seated need or desire to understand and represent God in some way, and that this need is closely connected to their moral and spiritual values.

The text also suggests that symbolizing God is a challenging task, because God is an experiential reality, meaning that he can only be truly known and understood through direct experience or encounter. This makes it difficult to represent God using symbols or images, because these symbols and images are necessarily limited and imperfect, and cannot fully capture the complexity and depth of the divine reality. The text suggests that this difficulty is inherent in the process of symbolizing God, and that it is something that mortal creatures must deal with in their attempts to represent the divine. Overall, the text is highlighting the complexities and challenges associated with symbolizing God, and is suggesting that this is an important and difficult task that is essential for human beings to undertake in their quest to understand and experience the divine.

0:2.2 (3.15) Cosmic consciousness implies the recognition of a First Cause, the one and only uncaused reality.

God, the Universal Father, functions on three Deity-personality levels of subinfinite value and relative divinity expression:

0:2.3 (3.16) 1. *Prepersonal*—as in the ministry of the Father fragments, such as the Thought Adjusters.

0:2.4 (3.17) 2. *Personal*—as in the evolutionary experience of created and procreated beings.

0:2.5 (3.18) 3. *Superpersonal*—as in the eventuated existences of certain absonite and associated beings.

The text is discussing the concept of cosmic consciousness, which is often used to refer to an expanded or heightened awareness of the universe and the various phenomena that exist within it. The text suggests that cosmic consciousness implies the recognition of a First Cause, which is the one and only uncaused reality – in other words, the thing or being that is the source or origin of all other things and beings. The text suggests that this First Cause is God, the Universal Father, who functions on three different levels of Deity-personality, each of which is associated with a specific type of divinity expression.

The first level of Deity-personality is prepersonal, and is associated with the ministry of the Father fragments, such as the Thought Adjusters. The second level of Deity-personality is personal, and is associated with the evolutionary experience of created and procreated beings. The third level of Deity-personality is superpersonal, and is associated with the eventuated existences of certain absonite and associated beings. The text suggests that these three levels of Deity-personality represent different ways in which God expresses his divinity and interacts with the universe and its inhabitants.

Overall, the text is suggesting that cosmic consciousness is closely connected to the concept of God, and that it involves an awareness of the First Cause and the various levels of Deity-personality that God functions on. The text is also highlighting the importance of recognizing and understanding these levels of Deity-personality in order to fully grasp the nature and significance of cosmic consciousness.

0:2.6 (3.19) GOD is a word symbol designating all personalizations of Deity. The term requires a different definition on each personal level of Deity function and must be still further redefined within each of these levels, as this term may be used to designate the diverse co-ordinate and subordinate personalizations of Deity; for example: the Paradise Creator Sons—the local universe fathers.

The text is discussing the concept of God, and is providing a definition of the term "God" as it is used in different contexts and in relation to different levels of Deity function. The text suggests that the term "God" is a word symbol that is used to designate all personalizations of Deity – in other words, all the different ways in which Deity can manifest as a personal being or entity. The text suggests that the meaning of the term "God" will vary depending on the specific level of Deity function that is being referred to, and that it may need to be further redefined within each of these levels in order to account for the diverse and complex ways in which Deity can be personalized.

For example, the text mentions the Paradise Creator Sons, who are sometimes referred to as the local universe fathers, and suggests that the term "God" may be used to designate these beings. This suggests that the term "God" can be applied to different personalizations of Deity on different levels of function, and that its meaning will vary depending on the specific context in which it is used. Overall, the text is highlighting the complex and multifaceted nature of the concept of God, and is suggesting that the term "God" must be carefully defined and understood in order to fully grasp its meaning and significance.

0:2.7 (4.1) The term God, as we make use of it, may be understood:

0:2.8 (4.2) *By designation*—as God the Father.

0:2.9 (4.3) *By context*—as when used in the discussion of

some one deity level or association. When in doubt as to the exact interpretation of the word God, it would be advisable to refer it to the person of the Universal Father.

The text is providing a definition of the term "God" as it is used in the context of the text. The text suggests that the term "God" can be understood in two different ways: first, by designation, as in the case of God the Father, and second, by context, as in the case of when the term is used in the discussion of some specific deity level or association. The text suggests that when in doubt about the exact interpretation of the word "God," it would be advisable to refer it to the person of the Universal Father, who is the source and ultimate embodiment of Deity.

Overall, the text is suggesting that the term "God" has a complex and multifaceted meaning, and that its interpretation will vary depending on the specific context in which it is used. The text is also emphasizing the centrality of the Universal Father in the concept of God, and is suggesting that the Father can serve as a reference point or starting point for understanding the meaning of the term "God" in different contexts.

0:2.10 (4.4) The term God always denotes *personality.* Deity may, or may not, refer to divinity personalities.

0:2.11 (4.5) The word GOD is used, in these papers, with the following meanings:

0:2.12 (4.6) 1. *God the Father*—Creator, Controller, and Upholder. The Universal Father, the First Person of Deity.

0:2.13 (4.7) 2. *God the Son*—Co-ordinate Creator, Spirit Controller, and Spiritual Administrator. The Eternal Son, the Second Person of Deity.

0:2.14 (4.8) 3. *God the Spirit*—Conjoint Actor, Universal Integrator, and Mind Bestower. The Infinite Spirit, the

Third Person of Deity.

0:2.15 (4.9) 4. *God the Supreme*—the actualizing or evolving God of time and space. Personal Deity associatively realizing the time-space experiential achievement of creature-Creator identity. The Supreme Being is personally experiencing the achievement of Deity unity as the evolving and experiential God of the evolutionary creatures of time and space.

0:2.16 (4.10) 5. *God the Sevenfold*—Deity personality anywhere actually functioning in time and space. The personal Paradise Deities and their creative associates functioning in and beyond the borders of the central universe and power-personalizing as the Supreme Being on the first creature level of unifying Deity revelation in time and space. This level, the grand universe, is the sphere of the time-space descension of Paradise personalities in reciprocal association with the time-space ascension of evolutionary creatures.

0:2.17 (4.11) 6. *God the Ultimate*—the eventuating God of supertime and transcended space. The second experiential level of unifying Deity manifestation. God the Ultimate implies the attained realization of the synthesized absonite-superpersonal, time-space-transcended, and eventuated-experiential values, co-ordinated on final creative levels of Deity reality.

0:2.18 (4.12) 7. *God the Absolute*—the experientializing God of transcended superpersonal values and divinity meanings, now existential as the *Deity Absolute*. This is the third level of unifying Deity expression and expansion. On this supercreative level, Deity experiences exhaustion of personalizable potential, encounters completion of divinity, and undergoes depletion of capacity for self-revelation to successive and progressive levels of other-personalization. Deity now encounters, impinges upon, and experiences identity with, the *Unqualified Absolute*.

The text is discussing the concept of God, and is providing a detailed explanation of the different ways in which the term "God" is used in the text. The text suggests that the term "God" always denotes personality, and that it is used to refer to personalizations of Deity. The text goes on to provide a list of seven different meanings or uses of the term "God" in the text, each of which corresponds to a different level or aspect of Deity function.

For example, the text suggests that the term "God" can be used to refer to the Universal Father, who is the First Person of Deity and the source of all that exists. The text also suggests that the term "God" can be used to refer to the

Eternal Son, who is the Second Person of Deity and co-ordinate Creator of the universe. The text further suggests that the term "God" can be used to refer to the Infinite Spirit, who is the Third Person of Deity and the universal integrator of all things.

Overall, the text is providing a rich and nuanced understanding of the concept of God, and is highlighting the complex and multifaceted nature of Deity and its many different aspects and functions. The text is also emphasizing the centrality of the Father, Son, and Spirit in the concept of God, and is suggesting that these three divine personalities are the fundamental basis of all that exists and all that is divine.

III. The First Source and Center

0:3.1 (4.13) Total, infinite reality is existential in seven phases and as seven co-ordinate Absolutes:

0:3.2 (5.1) 1. The First Source and Center.

0:3.3 (5.2) 2. The Second Source and Center.

0:3.4 (5.3) 3. The Third Source and Center.

0:3.5 (5.4) 4. The Isle of Paradise.

0:3.6 (5.5) 5. The Deity Absolute.

0:3.7 (5.6) 6. The Universal Absolute.

0:3.8 (5.7) 7. The Unqualified Absolute.

0:3.9 (5.8) God, as the First Source and Center, is primal in relation to total reality—unqualifiedly. The First Source and Center is infinite as well as eternal and is therefore limited or conditioned only by volition.

The text is discussing the concept of God as the First Source and Center of all reality, and is suggesting that God is primal, or fundamental, in relation to total reality. The text suggests that God is infinite and eternal, and is not limited or conditioned by anything other than his own volition. In other words, God is the ultimate source of all that exists, and is not subject to any external constraints or limitations.

The text is emphasizing the importance of the concept of God as the First Source and Center, and is suggesting that this concept is central to understanding the nature of reality and the universe as a whole. The text is also suggesting that God's status as the First Source and Center is unique and unparalleled, and that God is the ultimate source of all that exists and all that is divine. Overall, the text is providing a rich and expansive understanding of the concept of God, and is highlighting the central role that God plays in the universe and in the lives of all beings.

0:3.10 (5.9) God—the Universal Father—is the personality of the First Source and Center and as such maintains personal relations of infinite control over all co-ordinate and subordinate sources and centers. Such control is personal and infinite in *potential,* even though it may never actually function owing to the perfection of the function of such co-ordinate and subordinate sources and centers and personalities.

The text is discussing the concept of God as the Universal Father, and is suggesting that God is the personality of the First Source and Center. The text is emphasizing the personal nature of God, and is suggesting that God maintains personal relations of infinite control over all co-ordinate and subordinate sources and centers. In other words, God is not only the source of all that exists, but is also personally involved in the functioning and operation of the universe as a whole.

The text is also suggesting that God's control over the universe is infinite in potential, even though it may never actually be exercised due to the perfection of the function of other sources and centers within the universe. This suggests that God's power and control over the universe is not only immense, but also that it is ultimately limited by the inherent perfection and functioning of the universe itself.

Overall, the text is providing a rich and detailed understanding of the concept of God as the Universal Father, and is emphasizing the personal and controlling nature of God's relationship with the universe. The text is also suggesting that God's power and control over the universe is ultimately limited by the perfection and functioning of the universe itself, highlighting the complex and nuanced nature of God's role in the universe.

0:3.11 (5.10) The First Source and Center is, therefore, primal in all domains: deified or undeified, personal or impersonal, actual or potential, finite or infinite. No thing or being, no relativity or finality, exists except in direct or indirect relation to, and dependence on, the primacy of the First Source and Center.

The text is discussing the concept of the First Source and Center, and is suggesting that this concept is primal, or fundamental, in all domains of existence. The text is emphasizing that the First Source and Center is the ultimate source of all that exists, and that no thing or being, no matter how deified or undeified, personal or impersonal, actual or potential, finite or infinite, exists outside of its direct or indirect relation to and dependence on the First Source and Center.

In other words, the text is suggesting that the First Source and Center is the fundamental source of all that exists, and that everything that exists is ultimately dependent on the First Source and Center for its existence and its functioning. The text is emphasizing the all-encompassing nature of the First Source and Center, and is suggesting that it is the ultimate foundation of reality and the universe as a whole.

Overall, the text is providing a detailed and expansive understanding of the concept of the First Source and Center, and is highlighting the central and essential role that this concept plays in the universe and in the lives of all beings. The text is emphasizing the fundamental and primal nature of the First Source and Center, and is suggesting that it is the ultimate source of all that exists and all that is divine.

0:3.12 (5.11) **The First Source and Center** is related to the universe as:

0:3.13 (5.12) 1. The gravity forces of the material universes are convergent in the gravity center of nether Paradise. That is just why the geographic location of his person is eternally fixed in absolute relation to the force-energy center of the nether or material plane of Paradise. But the absolute personality of Deity exists on the upper or spiritual plane of Paradise.

0:3.14 (5.13) 2. The mind forces are convergent in the Infinite Spirit; the differential and divergent cosmic mind in the Seven Master Spirits; the factualizing mind of the Supreme as a time-space experience in Majeston.

0:3.15 (5.14) 3. The universe spirit forces are convergent in the Eternal Son.

0:3.16 (5.15) 4. The unlimited capacity for deity action

resides in the Deity Absolute.

0:3.17 (5.16) 5. The unlimited capacity for infinity response exists in the Unqualified Absolute.

0:3.18 (5.17) 6. The two Absolutes—Qualified and Unqualified—are co-ordinated and unified in and by the Universal Absolute.

0:3.19 (5.18) 7. The potential personality of an evolutionary moral being or of any other moral being is centered in the personality of the Universal Father.

The First Source and Center, also known as God or the Universal Father, is the primal source of all reality. It is the ultimate source of gravity, mind, and spirit forces in the universe, and is the ultimate source of deity action and infinity response. The First Source and Center is also the source of the potential personality of all moral beings, and is the center of all personal relationships with deity. The First

Source and Center is the origin and source of all that exists, and all things are in relation to and dependent on it.

0:3.20 (5.19) REALITY, as comprehended by finite beings, is partial, relative, and shadowy. The maximum Deity reality fully comprehensible by evolutionary finite creatures is embraced within the Supreme Being. Nevertheless there are antecedent and eternal realities, superfinite realities, which are ancestral to this Supreme Deity of evolutionary time-space creatures. In attempting to portray the origin and nature of universal reality, we are forced to employ the technique of time-space reasoning in order to reach the level of the finite mind. Therefore must many of the simultaneous events of eternity be presented as sequential transactions.

In simpler terms, reality as we know it is limited and incomplete. There are aspects of reality that are beyond our understanding and comprehension as finite beings. In order to discuss these concepts, we have to use time-based language and reasoning, even though many of these realities may not be bound by time.

0:3.21 (6.1) As a time-space creature would view the origin and differentiation of Reality, the eternal and infinite I AM achieved Deity liberation from the fetters of unqualified infinity through the exercise of inherent and eternal free will, and this divorcement from unqualified infinity produced the first *absolute divinity-tension*. This tension of infinity differential is resolved by the Universal Absolute, which functions to unify and co-ordinate the dynamic infinity of Total Deity and the static infinity of the Unqualified Absolute.

In other words, the concept of Reality has its origins in the eternal and infinite being known as the I AM. This being is able to exercise its own free will, which allows it to separate itself from the unqualified infinity of the universe. This separation creates a tension between the dynamic and static aspects of infinity, which is resolved through the actions of the Universal Absolute. This entity acts to unify and coordinate the two sides of infinity, creating a harmonious whole that is the basis for all of Reality.

0:3.22 (6.2) In this original transaction the theoretical I AM achieved the realization of personality by becoming the Eternal Father of the Original Son simultaneously with becoming the Eternal Source of the Isle of Paradise. Coexistent with the differentiation of the Son from the Father, and in the presence of Paradise, there appeared the person of the Infinite Spirit and the central universe of Havona. With the appearance of coexistent personal Deity, the Eternal Son and the Infinite Spirit, the Father escaped, as a personality, from otherwise inevitable diffusion throughout the potential of Total Deity. Thenceforth it is only in Trinity association with his two Deity equals that the Father fills all Deity potential, while increasingly experiential Deity is being actualized on the divinity levels of Supremacy, Ultimacy, and Absoluteness.

In this original transaction, the I AM, through the exercise of free will, became the Eternal Father and the Eternal Source of Paradise. As a result of this separation from unqualified infinity, the Son and the Spirit also appeared, allowing the Father to escape the otherwise inevitable diffusion throughout the potential of Total Deity. The Father, Son, and Spirit then formed the Trinity, working together to actualize experiential Deity on the levels of Supremacy, Ultimacy, and Absoluteness. These levels are characterized by the emergence of personality, the realization of time and space, and the transcendence of time and space, respectively.

0:3.23 (6.3) *The concept of the I AM* is a philosophic concession which we make to the time-bound, space-fettered, finite mind of man, to the impossibility of creature comprehension of eternity existences—nonbeginning, nonending realities and relationships. To the time-space creature, all things must have a beginning save only the ONE UNCAUSED—the primeval cause of causes. Therefore do we conceptualize this philosophic value-level as the I AM, at the same time instructing all creatures that the Eternal Son and the Infinite Spirit are coeternal with the I AM; in other words, that there never was a time when the I AM was not the *Father* of the Son and, with him, of the Spirit.

The concept of the I AM is a philosophical way of referring to the first and only uncaused reality, which is beyond the comprehension of finite, time-bound beings. This concept is used to help finite beings understand the concept of eternity and non-beginning, non-ending realities and relationships. The I AM is thought to be the primeval cause of all other causes, and is considered to be the source of the Eternal Son and the Infinite Spirit. These three beings are coeternal and have always existed together, with no beginning or end.

0:3.24 (6.4) ***The Infinite*** is used to denote the fullness—the finality—implied by the primacy of the First Source and Center. The *theoretical* I AM is a creature-philosophic extension of the "infinity of will," but the Infinite is an *actual* value-level representing the eternity-intension of the true infinity of the absolute and unfettered free will of the Universal Father. This concept is sometimes designated the Father-Infinite.

The concept of the Infinite is a way of describing the fullness and completeness of the First Source and Center, also known as the I AM. This concept is based on the idea of the "infinity of will," which refers to the unfettered free will of the Universal Father. This free will is eternal and absolute, and it is the source of all reality. The concept of the Infinite is used to describe the primacy of the First Source and Center and to convey the idea that this source is the ultimate source of all things. It is an actual value-level that represents the eternity-intension of the true infinity of the Universal Father's free will.

0:3.25 (6.5) Much of the confusion of all orders of beings, high and low, in their efforts to discover the Father-Infinite, is inherent in their limitations of comprehension. The absolute primacy of the Universal Father is not apparent on subinfinite levels; therefore is it probable that only the Eternal Son and the Infinite Spirit truly know the Father as an infinity; to all other personalities such a concept represents the exercise of faith.

The concept of the Father-Infinite refers to the eternal, uncaused nature of the Universal Father, the first source and center of all reality. This concept is difficult for finite beings to comprehend, as it goes beyond the limitations of time and space. Only the Eternal Son and the Infinite Spirit truly understand the Father as an infinity, while for all other beings, this concept requires faith to believe in. The concept of the Father-Infinite is important in understanding the nature of deity and the relationship between the Father and other divine beings.

IV. Universe Reality

0:4.1 (6.6) Reality differentially actualizes on diverse

universe levels; reality originates in and by the infinite volition of the Universal Father and is realizable in three primal phases on many different levels of universe actualization:

0:4.2 (6.7) 1. *Undeified reality* ranges from the energy domains of the nonpersonal to the reality realms of the nonpersonalizable values of universal existence, even to the presence of the Unqualified Absolute.

0:4.3 (7.1) 2. *Deified reality* embraces all infinite Deity potentials ranging upward through all realms of personality from the lowest finite to the highest infinite, thus encompassing the domain of all that which is personalizable and more—even to the presence of the Deity Absolute.

0:4.4 (7.2) 3. *Interassociated reality.* Universe reality is supposedly either deified or undeified, but to subdeified beings there exists a vast domain of interassociated reality, potential and actualizing, which is difficult of identification. Much of this co-ordinate reality is embraced within the realms of the Universal Absolute.

The concept of reality being divided into three phases is a way of describing the different levels or domains in which reality can exist or be experienced. The three phases are undeified reality, deified reality, and interassociated reality.

Undeified reality refers to the lower levels of reality, including the nonpersonal and nonpersonalizable realms of existence, such as energy and matter. These levels are not associated with deity or divinity and are characterized by their lack of personality.

Deified reality, on the other hand, refers to the higher levels of reality that are associated with deity and divinity. This includes all potentials of deity, from the lowest finite levels to the highest infinite levels, and encompasses all that is personalizable and beyond. This is the domain of personal and divine beings.

Interassociated reality is the domain of reality that is difficult to identify or define, as it lies between the other two phases. It is the realm of potential and actualizing co-ordinate reality, and is often associated with the Universal Absolute.

Overall, these three phases of reality help to explain the different levels or domains in which reality can exist or be experienced, and the way in which they are interconnected and related to each other.

0:4.5 (7.3) This is the primal concept of original reality: The Father initiates and maintains Reality. The primal *differentials* of reality are the deified and the undeified—the Deity Absolute and the Unqualified Absolute. The primal *relationship* is the tension between them. This Father-initiated divinity-tension is perfectly resolved by, and eternalizes as, the Universal Absolute.

The concept of original reality is based on the idea that the Universal Father, also known as the First Source and Center or the I AM, is the source of all reality. This includes both deified and undeified reality, which are two different categories of existence. Deified reality includes all things that are personalizable, or capable of having a personal aspect, and can be further divided into finite and infinite levels. Undeified reality, on the other hand, refers to nonpersonal and nonpersonalizable aspects of existence, such as energy and the presence of the Unqualified Absolute.

The tension between deified and undeified reality is resolved by the Universal Absolute, which unifies and coordinates these two aspects of existence. This concept of original reality suggests that the Universal Father is the initiator and sustainer of all reality, and that the tension between different aspects of existence is ultimately resolved by the Universal Absolute.

0:4.6 (7.4) From the viewpoint of time and space, reality is further divisible as:

0:4.7 (7.5) 1. *Actual and Potential.* Realities existing in fullness of expression in contrast to those which carry undisclosed capacity for growth. The Eternal Son is an absolute spiritual actuality; mortal man is very largely an unrealized spiritual potentiality.

0:4.8 (7.6) 2. *Absolute and Subabsolute.* Absolute realities are eternity existences. Subabsolute realities are projected on two levels: Absonites—realities which are relative with respect to both time and eternity. Finites—realities which are projected in space and are actualized in time.

0:4.9 (7.7) 3. *Existential and Experiential.* Paradise Deity is existential, but the emerging Supreme and Ultimate are experiential.

0:4.10 (7.8) 4. *Personal and Impersonal.* Deity expansion, personality expression, and universe evolution are forever conditioned by the Father's freewill act which forever separated the mind-spirit-personal meanings and values of actuality and potentiality centering in the Eternal Son from those things which center and inhere in the eternal Isle of Paradise.

In summary, the text is discussing the nature of reality and how it can be divided and understood. It emphasizes that God, or the First Source and Center, is the source of all reality and that reality can be divided into various categories such as actual and potential, absolute and subabsolute, and existential and experiential. It also discusses the tension between the deified and undeified aspects of reality and how it is resolved by the Universal Absolute.

0:4.11 (7.9) PARADISE is a term inclusive of the personal and the nonpersonal focal Absolutes of all phases of universe reality. Paradise, properly qualified, may connote any and all forms of reality, Deity, divinity, personality, and energy—spiritual, mindal, or material. All share Paradise as the place of origin, function, and destiny, as regards values, meanings, and factual existence.

Paradise is the source, center, and destiny of all that is real in the universe. It is the place where the personal and nonpersonal aspects of reality come together and interact. Paradise is the starting point for all forms of reality, including Deity, divinity, personality, and energy. It is the place where these elements come together and form the basis for the universe's values, meanings, and factual existence. Paradise is the ultimate destination for all beings, and it is where they will find the ultimate fulfillment of their potential.

0:4.12 (7.10) *The Isle of Paradise*—Paradise not otherwise qualified—is the Absolute of the material-gravity control of the First Source and Center. Paradise is motionless, being the only stationary thing in the universe of universes. The Isle of Paradise has a universe location but no position in space. This eternal Isle is the actual source of the physical universes—past, present, and future. The nuclear Isle of Light is a Deity derivative, but it is hardly Deity; neither are the material creations a part of Deity; they are a consequence.

The Isle of Paradise is a unique and fundamental aspect of the universe, with its own characteristics and properties that distinguish it from other parts of reality. It is the source of the material-gravity control of the First Source and Center, and therefore plays a central role in the functioning and evolution of the physical universe.

The Isle of Paradise is motionless, unlike the rest of the universe which is in constant motion and change. It also has a universe location, but does not have a position in space. This means that it exists within the universe, but is not bound by the same spatial limitations as other objects and entities.

The Isle of Paradise is also the source of the physical universes, meaning that it is the starting point from which all material things in the universe have originated. This includes all the galaxies, stars, planets, and other objects that make up the observable universe.

Overall, the Isle of Paradise is a unique and fundamental aspect of reality that is central to the functioning and evolution of the universe. It is a source of great power and significance, and plays a crucial role in the story of the universe and its inhabitants.

0:4.13 (7.11) Paradise is not a creator; it is a unique controller of many universe activities, far more of a controller than a reactor. Throughout the material universes Paradise influences the reactions and conduct of all beings having to do with force, energy, and power, but Paradise itself is unique, exclusive, and isolated in the universes. Paradise represents nothing and nothing represents Paradise. It is neither a force nor a presence; it is just *Paradise*.

Paradise, as the center of all gravity control in the material universes, is the source and destination of all physical matter and energy. As a unique and isolated controller, it influences the reactions and behavior of all beings and phenomena related to force, energy, and power. However,

Paradise itself is not a force or a presence, but rather a unique and exclusive reality. It is not a creator, but rather a controller of many universe activities. Despite its central role in the material universes, it is not considered a part of Deity, but rather a derivative of Deity. In this way, Paradise stands apart from the rest of the universe, both in terms of its origin and its function.

V. Personality Realities

0:5.1 (8.1) Personality is a level of deified reality and ranges from the mortal and midwayer level of the higher mind activation of worship and wisdom up through the morontial and spiritual to the attainment of finality of personality status. That is the evolutionary ascent of mortal- and kindred-creature personality, but there are numerous other orders of universe personalities.

Personality is a characteristic of living beings that allows for self-awareness, consciousness, and the ability to interact with the environment. It is a unique combination of individual characteristics, thoughts, emotions, and behavior that make up an individual's identity. Personality is a product of both nature and nurture, and can vary greatly from one person to another.

Personality is a fundamental aspect of reality, and exists on multiple levels in the universe. On the mortal and midwayer level, personality is associated with the higher mind and its ability to engage in worship and wisdom. As beings evolve and progress through the morontial and spiritual realms, their personalities become more refined and developed, ultimately attaining a level of finality.

In addition to the evolutionary ascent of mortal- and kindred-creature personalities, there are also numerous other orders of universe personalities. These may include divine beings, such as the Father, Son, and Spirit, as well as other beings with unique characteristics and abilities. The concept of personality is central to understanding the nature of the universe and the beings that inhabit it.

0:5.2 (8.2) Reality is subject to universal expansion, personality to infinite diversification, and both are capable of well-nigh unlimited Deity co-ordination and eternal stabilization. While the metamorphic range of nonpersonal reality is definitely limited, we know of no limitations to the progressive evolution of personality realities.

In summary, the text discusses the concept of God and its relation to cosmic consciousness, cosmic reality, and the evolution of mortal creatures. It explains that God, as the First Source and Center, is the primal source of all reality and is limited only by its own free will. God maintains personal relationships with all co-ordinate and subordinate sources and centers, and its presence can be found on various levels of reality, including the deified and undeified, the personal and impersonal, and the actual and potential. The text also discusses the concept of the I AM, which is a concession to the finite mind of man, and the Infinite, which is an actual value-level representing the eternity-intension of the true infinity of the Universal Father. Additionally, the text discusses the concept of Paradise and its relation to the control of universe activities, and the concept of personality and its potential for evolution and diversification.

0:5.3 (8.3) On attained experiential levels all personality orders or values are associable and even cocreational. Even God and man can coexist in a unified personality, as is so exquisitely demonstrated in the present status of Christ Michael—Son of Man and Son of God.

The text suggests that God and man can coexist in a unified personality, as demonstrated by Christ Michael, who is both the Son of Man and the Son of God. This concept suggests that it is possible for a finite, mortal being to achieve a level of unity and oneness with God, the infinite and eternal being who is the source of all reality. This unity may be realized through the attainment of certain spiritual qualities and states of being, such as worship and wisdom, and through the co-creation of reality with God.

0:5.4 (8.4) All subinfinite orders and phases of personality are associative attainables and are potentially cocreational. The prepersonal, the personal, and the superpersonal are all linked together by mutual potential of co-ordinate attainment, progressive achievement, and cocreational capacity. But never does the impersonal directly transmute to the personal. Personality is never spontaneous; it is the gift of the Paradise Father. Personality is superimposed upon energy, and it is associated only with living energy systems; identity can be associated with nonliving energy patterns.

The text discusses the relationship between personality and reality in the universe. It explains that while reality is subject to expansion and change, personality is characterized by infinite diversification and is capable of almost limitless coordination and stabilization by Deity. The text also notes that all orders of personality, from the lowest to the highest, are capable of association and co-creation with each other.

However, the text emphasizes that the impersonal cannot directly become the personal, and that personality is only possible in living energy systems.

0:5.5 (8.5) The Universal Father is the secret of the reality of personality, the bestowal of personality, and the destiny of personality. The Eternal Son is the absolute personality, the secret of spiritual energy, morontia spirits, and perfected spirits. The Conjoint Actor is the spirit-mind personality, the source of intelligence, reason, and the universal mind. But the Isle of Paradise is nonpersonal and extraspiritual, being the essence of the universal body, the source and center of physical matter, and the absolute master pattern of universal material reality.

The text is discussing the nature of reality and personality, as well as the roles of the three members of the Trinity (God the Father, the Eternal Son, and the Conjoint Actor) in relation to it. The Universal Father is said to be the source and bestower of personality, while the Eternal Son is the embodiment of absolute personality. The Conjoint Actor, also known as the Infinite Spirit, is the source of intelligence and reason, and is responsible for the universal mind. The Isle of Paradise, on the other hand, is nonpersonal and extraspiritual, being the source of physical matter and the master pattern of material reality. These entities work together to create and maintain reality, with the ultimate goal being the stabilization and co-ordination of all levels of personality and reality.

0:5.6 (8.6) These qualities of universal reality are

manifest in Urantian human experience on the following levels:

0:5.7 (8.7) 1. *Body.* The material or physical organism of man. The living electrochemical mechanism of animal nature and origin.

0:5.8 (8.8) 2. *Mind.* The thinking, perceiving, and feeling mechanism of the human organism. The total conscious and unconscious experience. The intelligence associated with the emotional life reaching upward through worship and wisdom to the spirit level.

0:5.9 (8.9) 3. *Spirit.* The divine spirit that indwells the mind of man—the Thought Adjuster. This immortal spirit is prepersonal—not a personality, though destined to become a part of the personality of the surviving mortal creature.

0:5.10 (8.10) 4. *Soul.* The soul of man is an experiential acquirement. As a mortal creature chooses to "do the will of the Father in heaven," so the indwelling spirit becomes the father of a *new reality* in human experience. The mortal and material mind is the mother of this same emerging reality. The substance of this new reality is neither material nor spiritual—it is *morontial.* This is the emerging and immortal soul which is destined to survive mortal death and begin the Paradise ascension.

0:5.11 (9.1) *Personality.* The personality of mortal man is neither body, mind, nor spirit; neither is it the soul. Personality is the one changeless reality in an otherwise ever-changing creature experience; and it unifies all other associated factors of individuality. The personality is the unique bestowal which the Universal Father makes upon the living and associated energies of matter, mind, and spirit, and which survives with the survival of the morontial soul.

0:5.12 (9.2) *Morontia* is a term designating a vast level intervening between the material and the spiritual. It may designate personal or impersonal realities, living or nonliving energies. The warp of morontia is spiritual; its woof is physical.

The text describes the various aspects of human experience and how they relate to universal reality. The body is the material or physical organism of a person. The mind is the thinking, perceiving, and feeling mechanism of the human organism. The spirit is the divine spirit that indwells the mind of a person, and the soul is the experiential acquirement that results from choosing to do the will of God. Personality is the unique bestowal that the Universal Father makes upon the living and associated energies of matter, mind, and spirit, and it survives with the survival of the morontial soul. Morontia is a level between the material and the spiritual, and it can refer to personal or impersonal realities, living or nonliving energies.

VI. Energy and Pattern

0:6.1 (9.3) Any and all things responding to the personality circuit of the Father, we call personal. Any and all things responding to the spirit circuit of the Son, we call spirit. Any and all that responds to the mind circuit of the Conjoint Actor, we call mind, mind as an attribute of the Infinite Spirit—mind in all its phases. Any and all that responds to the material-gravity circuit centering in nether Paradise, we call matter—energy-matter in all its metamorphic states.

The text suggests that certain concepts and phenomena in the universe can be understood and classified based on their relationship to the three main elements of reality: the Universal Father (who represents personality), the Eternal Son (who represents spirit), and the Conjoint Actor (who represents mind). The text also describes how these three elements can be further divided into levels, such as the personal and impersonal, the actual and potential, and the existential and experiential. Additionally, the text suggests that the concept of "morontia" encompasses a level of reality that lies between the material and spiritual realms.

0:6.2 (9.4) ENERGY we use as an all-inclusive term applied to spiritual, mindal, and material realms. *Force* is also thus broadly used. *Power* is ordinarily limited to the designation of the electronic level of material or linear-gravity-responsive matter in the grand universe. Power is also employed to designate sovereignty. We cannot follow your generally accepted definitions of force, energy, and power. There is such paucity of language that we must assign multiple meanings to these terms.

In this text, "energy" is used as a broad term to refer to any kind of action or activity that takes place in the spiritual, mental, or material realms. "Force" is also used in a broad sense, as a term that encompasses any kind of power or influence that can be exerted on something else. "Power" is typically used to refer specifically to the electronic level of material or linear-gravity-responsive matter in the universe. It can also refer to sovereignty or control. The language used in the text is somewhat flexible and open to multiple interpretations, which can lead to confusion.

0:6.3 (9.5) *Physical energy* is a term denoting all phases and forms of phenomenal motion, action, and potential.

0:6.4 (9.6) In discussing physical-energy manifestations, we generally use the terms cosmic force, emergent energy, and universe power. These are often employed as follows:

0:6.5 (9.7) 1. *Cosmic force* embraces all energies deriving from the Unqualified Absolute but which are as yet unresponsive to Paradise gravity.

0:6.6 (9.8) 2. *Emergent energy* embraces those energies which are responsive to Paradise gravity but are as yet unresponsive to local or linear gravity. This is the pre-electronic level of energy-matter.

0:6.7 (9.9) 3. *Universe power* includes all forms of energy which, while still responding to Paradise gravity, are directly responsive to linear gravity. This is the electronic level of energy-matter and all subsequent evolutions thereof.

0:6.8 (9.10) *Mind* is a phenomenon connoting the presence-activity of *living ministry* in addition to varied energy systems; and this is true on all levels of intelligence. In personality, mind ever intervenes between spirit and matter; therefore is the universe illuminated by three kinds of light: material light, intellectual insight, and spirit luminosity.

0:6.9 (10.1) *Light*—spirit luminosity—is a word symbol, a figure of speech, which connotes the personality manifestation characteristic of spirit beings of diverse orders. This luminous emanation is in no respect related either to intellectual insight or to physical-light manifestations.

The text describes the different aspects of reality and their relationship to each other. It discusses the concept of the "I AM" and its relationship to the Eternal Son and the Infinite Spirit. It also talks about the nature of personality and its connection to the Universal Father, the Eternal Son, and the Conjoint Actor. The text also explains the different levels of reality, including undeified and deified, absolute and subabsolute, existential and experiential, and personal and impersonal. It also discusses the concept of Paradise, its nature and relationship to the universe, and the different aspects of human experience, such as body, mind, spirit, soul, personality, and morontia. Finally, the text discusses the concept of energy and its different forms and levels, including cosmic force, emergent energy, and universe power.

0:6.10 (10.2) PATTERN can be projected as material, spiritual, or mindal, or any combination of these energies. It can pervade personalities, identities, entities, or nonliving matter. But pattern is pattern and remains pattern; only *copies* are multiplied.

A pattern can be thought of as a blueprint or a model that serves as a guide or template for creating something. In the context of the above text, the word "pattern" is being used to refer to a model or guide for creating various forms of reality, such as material, spiritual, or mental realities. This suggests that patterns are not necessarily limited to physical objects, but can also be applied to other forms of existence. Furthermore, the text implies that patterns are fixed and unchanging, and that only copies or replicas of them can be created. This suggests that patterns serve as a basis or foundation for creating new things, but do not themselves change or evolve.

0:6.11 (10.3) Pattern may configure energy, but it does not control it. Gravity is the sole control of energy-matter. Neither space nor pattern are gravity responsive, but there is no relationship between space and pattern;

space is neither pattern nor potential pattern. Pattern is a configuration of reality which has already paid all gravity debt; the *reality* of any pattern consists of its energies, its mind, spirit, or material components.

In other words, pattern is a characteristic of reality that influences the arrangement and organization of energy, but it does not have the ability to control it. Gravity is the only force that has control over energy-matter. Additionally, while space and pattern may have some relationship, they are not the same thing. Space is not a pattern or a potential pattern. Rather, pattern is a specific configuration of reality that is made up of its various energy, mind, spirit, or material components.

0:6.12 (10.4) In contrast to the aspect of the *total*, pattern discloses the *individual* aspect of energy and of personality. Personality or identity forms are patterns resultant from energy (physical, spiritual, or mindal) but are not inherent therein. That quality of energy or of personality by virtue of which pattern is caused to appear may be attributed to God—Deity—to Paradise force endowment, to the coexistence of personality and power.

The concept of pattern is used to describe a specific arrangement or configuration of energy or personality. This arrangement or configuration is distinct from the energy or personality itself, but it is a result of it. For example, the pattern of a person's thoughts and behaviors may be seen as a result of the person's energy and personality. Pattern is a way of understanding the individual aspects of energy and personality, rather than their overall nature. It is a way of examining the specific arrangements and configurations that arise from these fundamental components of reality.

0:6.13 (10.5) Pattern is a master design from which copies are made. Eternal Paradise is the absolute of patterns; the Eternal Son is the pattern personality; the Universal Father is the direct ancestor-source of both. But Paradise does not bestow pattern, and the Son cannot bestow personality.

The text is discussing the concept of pattern and its relationship to other elements of the universe. It states that pattern is a configuration of reality that has already paid its gravity debt, and that it is a master design from which copies are made. The text also describes how pattern is related to other elements of the universe, such as energy, personality, and God. It suggests that pattern is caused to appear by the presence of God, or by the coexistence of personality and power. Overall, the text suggests that pattern is a fundamental aspect of the universe and is closely connected to other important elements such as energy, personality, and God.

VII. The Supreme Being

0:7.1 (10.6) The Deity mechanism of the master universe is twofold as concerns eternity relationships. God the Father, God the Son, and God the Spirit are eternal—are existential beings—while God the Supreme, God the Ultimate, and God the Absolute are *actualizing* Deity personalities of the post-Havona epochs in the time-space and the time-space-transended spheres of master universe evolutionary expansion. These actualizing Deity personalities are future eternals from the time when, and as, they power-personalize in the growing universes by the technique of the experiential actualization of the associative-creative potentials of the eternal Paradise Deities.

0:7.2 (10.7) Deity is, therefore, dual in presence:

0:7.3 (10.8) 1. *Existential*—beings of eternal existence, past, present, and future.

0:7.4 (10.9) 2. *Experiential*—beings actualizing in the post-Havona present but of unending existence throughout all future eternity.

The text explains that Deity, or God, exists in two forms: existential and experiential. Existential Deity refers to beings that have existed for all eternity, and will continue to exist for all eternity. This includes God the Father, God the Son, and God the Spirit. Experiential Deity, on the other hand, refers to beings that are still in the process of actualizing, or coming into being, in the post-Havona present. These beings will also have unending existence throughout all future eternity, but they are not yet fully realized. Examples of experiential Deity include God the Supreme, God the Ultimate, and God the Absolute.

0:7.5 (10.10) The Father, Son, and Spirit are existential—existential in actuality (though all potentials are supposedly experiential). The Supreme and the Ultimate are wholly experiential. The Deity

Absolute is experiential in actualization but existential in potentiality. The essence of Deity is eternal, but only the three original persons of Deity are unqualifiedly eternal. All other Deity personalities have an origin, but they are eternal in destiny.

The concept of Deity being dual in presence refers to the existence of two types of Deity: existential and experiential. Existential Deity refers to the three original persons of Deity: the Father, the Son, and the Spirit. These beings are eternal, with no beginning or end to their existence. Experiential Deity, on the other hand, refers to Deity personalities that have come into being through the experiential actualization of the potentials of the eternal Paradise Deities. Examples of experiential Deity include the Supreme and the Ultimate, which are actualizing in the post-Havona present. While they have an origin, they are eternal in destiny. The Deity Absolute is also experiential in actualization but existential in potentiality. Overall, the duality of Deity presence highlights the eternal nature of Deity, as well as its potential for growth and evolution through the experiential actualization of its potentials.

0:7.6 (10.11) Having achieved existential Deity expression of himself in the Son and the Spirit, the Father is now achieving experiential expression on hitherto impersonal and unrevealed deity levels as God the Supreme, God the Ultimate, and God the Absolute; but these experiential Deities are not now fully existent; they are in process of actualization.

The text is referring to the three aspects of Deity – the

Father, the Son, and the Spirit – and how they are related to the concept of existence. According to the text, the Father, Son, and Spirit are "existential" in that they are actual beings with eternal existence. In contrast, other Deity personalities, such as God the Supreme, God the Ultimate, and God the Absolute, are considered "experiential" in that they are in the process of actualization. This means that while these Deity personalities are not yet fully existent, they are on a path towards eternal existence.

0:7.7 (11.1) *God the Supreme* in Havona is the personal spirit reflection of the triune Paradise Deity. This associative Deity relationship is now creatively expanding outward in God the Sevenfold and is synthesizing in the experiential power of the Almighty Supreme in the grand universe. Paradise Deity, existential as three persons, is thus experientially evolving in two phases of Supremacy, while these dual phases are power-personality unifying as one Lord, the Supreme Being.

The concept of God in this text refers to the Universal Father, who is the primary personality of the triune Paradise Deity. This deity consists of three persons, the Father, the Son, and the Spirit. The Father initiates and maintains reality, and is the source of all that is personal. The Son is the absolute personality, and the source of spiritual energy and perfected spirits. The Spirit is the source of intelligence and the universal mind.

The text also discusses the evolution of God in two phases of Supremacy, which refer to the evolution of God the Supreme in Havona and the Almighty Supreme in the grand universe. These phases represent the expansion and synthesis of the Paradise Deity as it evolves into a more complex and powerful being. This evolution is also known as the experiential power-personality unification of the

Supreme Being.

0:7.8 (11.2) The Universal Father achieves freewill liberation from the bonds of infinity and the fetters of eternity by the technique of trinitization, threefold Deity personalization. The Supreme Being is even now evolving as a subeternal personality unification of the sevenfold manifestation of Deity in the time-space segments of the grand universe.

The Universal Father is the source of all reality and the creator of all things. He achieves his own freedom and individuality by trinitizing, or manifesting himself as three distinct personalities: the Father, the Son, and the Spirit. These three personalities work together to create and maintain the universe. The Supreme Being is a future evolution of these personalities, representing the culmination of their efforts in the time-space segments of the grand universe. This Supreme Being is a powerful, personal deity who is the synthesis of the sevenfold manifestation of Deity, and is capable of unifying all aspects of reality into one cohesive whole.

0:7.9 (11.3) *The Supreme Being* is not a direct creator, except that he is the father of Majeston, but he is a synthetic co-ordinator of all creature-Creator universe activities. The Supreme Being, now actualizing in the evolutionary universes, is the Deity correlator and synthesizer of time-space divinity, of triune Paradise Deity in experiential association with the Supreme Creators of time and space. When finally actualized, this evolutionary Deity will constitute the eternal fusion of the finite and the infinite—the everlasting and indissoluble union of experiential power and spirit personality.

The text suggests that the Supreme Being is a Deity that is in the process of actualization. This process involves the synthesis of time-space divinity, or the combination of the finite and the infinite, with the triune Paradise Deity. The Supreme Being is not a direct creator, but acts as a coordinator of all creature-Creator activities in the universe. Once fully actualized, the Supreme Being will be the eternal fusion of finite and infinite, power and spirit personality.

0:7.10 (11.4) All time-space finite reality, under the directive urge of the evolving Supreme Being, is engaged in an ever-ascending mobilization and perfecting unification (power-personality synthesis) of all phases and values of finite reality, in association with varied phases of Paradise reality, to the end and for the purpose of subsequently embarking upon the attempt to reach absonite levels of supercreature attainment.

The text describes the Supreme Being as a Deity that is evolving in the time-space segments of the grand universe. The Supreme Being is a synthesis of the sevenfold manifestation of Deity and is a co-ordinator of all creature-Creator universe activities. As the Supreme Being continues to evolve, it is unifying and perfecting all phases and values of finite reality in association with phases of Paradise reality. This is done with the ultimate goal of reaching absonite levels of supercreature attainment.

VIII. God the Sevenfold

0:8.1 (11.5) To atone for finity of status and to compensate for creature limitations of concept, the Universal Father has established the evolutionary creature's sevenfold approach to Deity:

0:8.2 (11.6) 1. The Paradise Creator Sons.

0:8.3 (11.7) 2. The Ancients of Days.

0:8.4 (11.8) 3. The Seven Master Spirits.

0:8.5 (11.9) 4. The Supreme Being.

0:8.6 (11.10) 5. God the Spirit.

0:8.7 (11.11) 6. God the Son.

0:8.8 (11.12) 7. God the Father.

The sevenfold approach to Deity allows for the gradual understanding and comprehension of the nature of God by evolutionary creatures. This approach is made possible by the existence of various levels and phases of Deity, each providing a different perspective and understanding of the nature of God. The Paradise Creator Sons, for example, are personal representatives of the Father and help to reveal his nature and will to the universe. The Ancients of Days, on the other hand, are judicial rulers and help to maintain order and justice throughout the universe. The Seven Master Spirits, meanwhile, are the administrators of the universe and help to oversee its functioning. The Supreme Being, God the Spirit, God the Son, and God the Father represent increasingly profound levels of Deity, allowing for a deeper understanding of the nature of God. Together, these levels and phases of Deity provide a comprehensive approach to understanding the nature of the Universal Father.

0:8.9 (11.13) This sevenfold Deity personalization in time and space and to the seven superuniverses enables mortal man to attain the presence of God, who is spirit. This sevenfold Deity, to finite time-space creatures sometime power-personalizing in the Supreme Being, is the functional Deity of the mortal evolutionary creatures of the Paradise-ascension career. Such an experiential discovery-career of the realization of God begins with the recognition of the divinity of the Creator Son of the local universe and ascends through the superuniverse Ancients of Days and by way of the person of one of the Seven Master Spirits to the attainment of the discovery and recognition of the divine personality of the Universal Father on Paradise.

The sevenfold approach to Deity allows for finite beings to progress towards a fuller understanding and experience of God. This progression begins with the recognition of the divinity of the Creator Son in the local universe, and continues through the recognition of the superuniverse Ancients of Days and the Seven Master Spirits. Ultimately, this progression leads to the discovery and recognition of the divine personality of the Universal Father on Paradise. This sevenfold approach allows for a functional understanding of Deity for mortal evolutionary creatures pursuing the Paradise-ascension career.

0:8.10 (12.1) The grand universe is the threefold Deity domain of the Trinity of Supremacy, God the Sevenfold, and the Supreme Being. God the Supreme is potential in the Paradise Trinity, from whom he derives his personality and spirit attributes; but he is now actualizing in the Creator Sons, Ancients of Days, and the Master Spirits, from whom he derives his power as Almighty to the superuniverses of time and space.

The grand universe is the domain of three aspects of the deity: the Trinity of Supremacy, God the Sevenfold, and the Supreme Being. The Trinity of Supremacy is the potential for the Supreme Being, from whom the Supreme Being derives its personality and spirit attributes. The Sevenfold is the actualization of the Supreme Being in the Creator Sons, Ancients of Days, and Master Spirits, from whom the Supreme Being derives its power as Almighty over the superuniverses of time and space. These three aspects of deity work together to enable mortal creatures to attain the presence of God and to embark on the Paradise-ascension career.

This power manifestation of the immediate God of evolutionary creatures actually time-space evolves concomitantly with them. The Almighty Supreme, evolving on the value-level of nonpersonal activities, and the spirit person of God the Supreme are *one reality*—the Supreme Being.

The Supreme Being is the unity of God the Supreme, the Almighty Supreme, and the spirit person of God the Supreme. This unity represents the manifestation of the power and personality of the immediate God of evolutionary creatures in time and space. As such, the Supreme Being evolves concomitantly with these creatures, growing and developing along with them. The Supreme Being is not a direct creator, but rather a synthesizer and coordinator of the activities of the universe, guiding the evolution of all beings towards higher levels of understanding and unity with the divine.

0:8.11 (12.2) The Creator Sons in the Deity association of God the Sevenfold provide the mechanism whereby the mortal becomes immortal and the finite attains the embrace of the infinite. The Supreme Being provides the technique for the power-personality mobilization, the divine synthesis, of *all* these manifold transactions, thus enabling the finite to attain the absonite and, through other possible future actualizations, to attempt the attainment of the Ultimate. The Creator Sons and their associated Divine Ministers are participants in this supreme mobilization, but the Ancients of Days and the Seven Master Spirits are probably eternally fixed as permanent administrators in the grand universe.

The text is discussing the different levels of Deity in the grand universe and how they relate to one another. The grand universe is said to be the domain of the Trinity of Supremacy, which consists of God the Sevenfold, the Supreme Being, and the three original persons of the Paradise Trinity (God the Father, God the Son, and God the Spirit). The Creator Sons and their associated Divine Ministers are said to provide the mechanism for mortal beings to become immortal and finite beings to attain the embrace of the infinite. The Supreme Being is described as the technique for the power-personality mobilization, or synthesis, of all these transactions, allowing finite beings to

attain the absonite and potentially even the Ultimate. The
Ancients of Days and the Seven Master Spirits are said to be
fixed as permanent administrators in the grand universe.

0:8.12 (12.3) The function of God the Sevenfold dates from the organization of the seven superuniverses, and it will probably expand in connection with the future evolution of the creations of outer space. The organization of these future universes of the primary, secondary, tertiary, and quartan space levels of progressive evolution will undoubtedly witness the inauguration of the transcendent and absonite approach to Deity.

God the Sevenfold is a manifestation of the triune Paradise
Deity, which includes God the Father, God the Son, and God

the Spirit. This sevenfold manifestation of Deity is present in the seven superuniverses of the grand universe and is involved in the evolutionary development of time and space. The function of God the Sevenfold is to enable mortal creatures to attain a relationship with the divine and to eventually attain immortality and embrace the infinite. This is accomplished through the Creator Sons and their associated Divine Ministers, who are involved in the mobilization of power and personality in the grand universe. The organization of future universes may also involve the transcendent and absonite approach to Deity.

IX. God the Ultimate

0:9.1 (12.4) Just as the Supreme Being progressively evolves from the antecedent divinity endowment of the encompassed grand universe potential of energy and personality, so does God the Ultimate eventuate from the potentials of divinity residing in the transcended time-space domains of the master universe. The actualization of Ultimate Deity signalizes absonite unification of the first experiential Trinity and signifies unifying Deity expansion on the second level of creative self-realization. This constitutes the personality-power equivalent of the universe experiential-Deity actualization of Paradise absonite realities on the eventuating levels of transcended time-space values. The completion of such an experiential unfoldment is designed to afford ultimate service-destiny for all time-space creatures who have attained absonite levels through the completed realization of the Supreme Being and by the ministry of God the Sevenfold.

The text discusses the concept of Deity and how it relates to the grand universe. It explains that the function of God the Sevenfold is to provide a mechanism for mortal creatures to become immortal and finite beings to attain the embrace of the infinite. The Supreme Being is described as providing the technique for the power-personality mobilization of all these transactions, enabling finite beings to attain the absonite and potentially even the Ultimate. The text also mentions the potential evolution of future universes and the potential inauguration of the transcendent and absonite approach to Deity.

0:9.2 (12.5) *God the Ultimate* is designative of personal Deity functioning on the divinity levels of the absonite and on the universe spheres of supertime and transcended space. The Ultimate is a supersupreme eventuation of Deity. The Supreme is the Trinity unification comprehended by finite beings; the Ultimate is the unification of the Paradise Trinity comprehended by absonite beings.

God the Ultimate is a concept that represents the evolution of the Supreme Being, a personal manifestation of the triune Paradise Deity, into an even higher form of deity that is comprehended by beings that exist on the absonite level. The Ultimate is the result of the unity of the Paradise Trinity and its expansion into new levels of existence that transcend time and space. This concept suggests that there *are higher levels of deity beyond what finite beings can comprehend, and that these higher levels are the destination for beings who have achieved the completion of the Supreme Being and have been ministered to by God the Sevenfold.*

0:9.3 (13.1) The Universal Father, through the mechanism of evolutionary Deity, is actually engaged in the stupendous and amazing *act* of personality focalization and power mobilization, on their respective universe meaning-levels, of the divine reality values of the finite, the absonite, and even of the absolute.

The text discusses the concept of universal reality and its manifestation in human experience on various levels. These levels include the body, mind, spirit, soul, personality, and morontia. The text also mentions the concept of energy, which is used as an all-inclusive term applied to the spiritual, mindal, and material realms. It also mentions the concept of pattern, which is a master design from which copies are made, and the concept of Deity, which is twofold in terms of eternity relationships. The text also discusses the concept of the Supreme Being, which is the personal spirit reflection of the triune Paradise Deity and is actualizing in the time-space segments of the grand universe.

0:9.4 (13.2) The first three and past-eternal Deities of Paradise—the Universal Father, the Eternal Son, and the Infinite Spirit—are, in the eternal future, to be personality-complemented by the experiential actualization of associate evolutionary Deities—God the Supreme, God the Ultimate, and possibly God the

Absolute.

The text suggests that the Universal Father, the Eternal Son, and the Infinite Spirit are eternal beings that have always existed. However, there are other Deities that are in the process of being "actualized" through the experience of evolutionary creatures. These Deities include God the Supreme, God the Ultimate, and possibly God the Absolute. The text implies that these experiential Deities will eventually attain full existence and complement the original three Deities of Paradise in the eternal future.

0:9.5 (13.3) God the Supreme and God the Ultimate, now evolving in the experiential universes, are not existential—not past eternals, only future eternals, time-space-conditioned and transcendental-conditioned eternals. They are Deities of supreme, ultimate, and possibly supreme-ultimate endowments, but they have experienced historic universe origins. They will never have an end, but they do have personality beginnings. They are indeed actualizations of eternal and infinite Deity potentials, but they themselves are neither unqualifiedly eternal nor infinite.

In other words, God the Supreme and God the Ultimate are not eternal beings like the Father, Son, and Spirit, but rather beings that have evolved over time in the experiential universes. They have beginnings but no end, and while they possess supreme and ultimate endowments, they are not infinite like the original three Deities of Paradise. These evolving Deities are a manifestation of the potential of eternal and infinite Deity, but they are not eternal and infinite themselves.

X. God the Absolute

0:10.1 (13.4) There are many features of the eternal reality of the *Deity Absolute* which cannot be fully explained to the time-space finite mind, but the actualization of *God the Absolute* would be in consequence of the unification of the second experiential Trinity, the Absolute Trinity. This would constitute the experiential realization of absolute divinity, the unification of absolute meanings on absolute levels; but we are not certain regarding the encompassment of all absolute values since we have at no time been informed that the Qualified Absolute is the equivalent of the Infinite. Superultimate destinies are involved in absolute meanings and infinite spirituality, and without both of these unachieved realities we cannot establish absolute values.

The concept of the Deity Absolute is a complex one that is difficult to fully understand from a time-space finite perspective. The Absolute is a potential Deity that is the result of the unification of the second experiential Trinity, which is made up of God the Supreme, God the Ultimate, and potentially God the Absolute. This unification of the Absolute Trinity would constitute the experiential realization of absolute divinity, the unification of absolute meanings on absolute levels. However, it is uncertain whether this would encompass all absolute values, as it is not known whether the Qualified Absolute is equivalent to the Infinite. The concept of the Absolute implies the involvement of superultimate destinies and the need for both unachieved absolute values and infinite spirituality.

0:10.2 (13.5) God the Absolute is the realization-attainment goal of all superabsonite beings, but the power and personality potential of the Deity Absolute transcends our concept, and we hesitate to discuss those realities which are so far removed from experiential actualization.

The concept of God the Absolute, as mentioned in the text, seems to refer to a potential future realization of deity. This realization would be the result of the unification of the second experiential Trinity, known as the Absolute Trinity. This Absolute Trinity would constitute the experiential realization of absolute divinity, unifying absolute meanings on absolute levels. However, the text also mentions that the concept of God the Absolute is difficult to fully explain to time-space finite minds, and that its power and personality potential may transcend our understanding. It is also noted that superultimate destinies may be involved in the realization of absolute values, but without achieving these values, it is not possible to establish absolute meanings.

XI. The Three Absolutes

0:11.1 (13.6) When the combined thought of the Universal Father and the Eternal Son, functioning in the God of Action, constituted the creation of the divine and central universe, the Father followed the expression of his thought into the word of his Son and the act of their Conjoint Executive by differentiating his Havona presence from the potentials of infinity. And these undisclosed infinity potentials remain space concealed in the Unqualified Absolute and divinely enshrouded in the Deity Absolute, while these two become one in the functioning of the Universal Absolute, the unrevealed infinity-unity of the Paradise Father.

The text is discussing the creation of the universe, specifically the Havona universe, which is the central and divine universe of the grand universe. The Universal Father and the Eternal Son, together known as the God of Action, created Havona and the Father followed the expression of his thought into the word of his Son and the act of their Conjoint Executive. The text also mentions the potentials of infinity and how they remain space concealed in the Unqualified Absolute and divinely enshrouded in the Deity Absolute. The Universal Absolute is the unrevealed infinity-

unity of the Paradise Father.

0:11.2 (13.7) Both potency of cosmic force and potency of spirit force are in process of progressive revelation-realization as the enrichment of all reality is effected by experiential growth and through the correlation of the experiential with the existential by the Universal Absolute. By virtue of the equipoising presence of the Universal Absolute, the First Source and Center realizes extension of experiential power, enjoys identification with his evolutionary creatures, and achieves expansion of experiential Deity on the levels of Supremacy, Ultimacy, and Absoluteness.

The concept of the Universal Absolute is tied to the idea of the progression and evolution of reality. The Universal

Absolute represents the potential for the unification and realization of both cosmic force (energy) and spirit force, which are in a state of revelation and growth through experience. This unification and realization allows for the expansion of experiential power and Deity, as well as the ability for the First Source and Center (God) to be connected and identified with its evolutionary creatures. In this way, the Universal Absolute is a key concept in understanding the ongoing progression and evolution of reality.

0:11.3 (14.1) When it is not possible fully to distinguish the Deity Absolute from the Unqualified Absolute, their supposedly combined function or co-ordinated presence is designated the action of the Universal Absolute.

0:11.4 (14.2) 1. *The Deity Absolute* seems to be the all-powerful activator, while the Unqualified Absolute appears to be the all-efficient mechanizer of the supremely unified and ultimately co-ordinated universe of universes, even universes upon universes, made, making, and yet to be made.

0:11.5 (14.3) The Deity Absolute cannot, or at least does not, react to any universe situation in a subabsolute manner. Every response of this Absolute to any given situation appears to be made in terms of the welfare of the whole creation of things and beings, not only in its present state of existence, but also in view of the infinite possibilities of all future eternity.

0:11.6 (14.4) The Deity Absolute is that potential which was segregated from total, infinite reality by the freewill choice of the Universal Father, and within which all divinity activities—existential and experiential—take place. This is the *Qualified Absolute* in contradistinction to the *Unqualified Absolute*; but the Universal Absolute is superadditive to both in the encompassment of all absolute potential.

0:11.7 (14.5) 2. *The Unqualified Absolute* is nonpersonal, extradivine, and undeified. The Unqualified Absolute is therefore devoid of personality, divinity, and all creator prerogatives. Neither fact nor truth, experience nor revelation, philosophy nor absonity are able to penetrate the nature and character of this Absolute without universe qualification.

0:11.8 (14.6) Let it be made clear that the Unqualified Absolute is a *positive reality* pervading the grand universe and, apparently, extending with equal space presence on out into the force activities and prematerial evolutions of the staggering stretches of the space regions beyond the seven superuniverses. The Unqualified Absolute is not a mere negativism of philosophic concept predicated on the assumptions of metaphysical sophistries concerning the universality, dominance, and primacy of the unconditioned and the unqualified. The Unqualified Absolute is a positive universe overcontrol in infinity; this overcontrol is space-force unlimited but is definitely conditioned by the presence of life, mind, spirit, and personality, and is further conditioned by the will-reactions and purposeful mandates of the Paradise Trinity.

0:11.9 (14.7) We are convinced that the Unqualified Absolute is not an undifferentiated and all-pervading influence comparable either to the pantheistic concepts of metaphysics or to the sometime ether hypothesis of science. The Unqualified Absolute is force unlimited and Deity conditioned, but we do not fully perceive the relation of this Absolute to the spirit realities of the universes.

0:11.10 (14.8) 3. *The Universal Absolute,* we logically deduce, was inevitable in the Universal Father's absolute freewill act of differentiating universe realities into deified and undeified—personalizable and nonpersonalizable—values. The Universal Absolute is the Deity phenomenon indicative of the resolution of the tension created by the freewill act of thus differentiating universe reality, and functions as the associative co-ordinator of these sum totals of existential potentialities.

0:11.11 (15.1) The tension-presence of the Universal Absolute signifies the adjustment of differential between deity reality and undeified reality inherent in the separation of the dynamics of freewill divinity from the statics of unqualified infinity.

The text discusses the concept of the Deity Absolute, which is a type of Deity or divine being that is part of the universe's fundamental structure. The text explains that the Deity Absolute is a combination of the Deity Absolute and the Unqualified Absolute, which are two aspects of the universe that are not fully understood by time-space finite beings. The text also explains that the Universal Absolute is the result of the tension created by the freewill act of differentiating universe reality into deified and undeified values. This means that the Universal Absolute is the co-ordinator of these potentialities, and its presence signifies the adjustment of the difference between deity reality and undeified reality. Overall, the text suggests that the Deity Absolute, the Unqualified Absolute, and the Universal Absolute are all related to the fundamental structure of the universe and the relationship between deity and undeified reality.

0:11.12 (15.2) Always remember: Potential infinity is absolute and inseparable from eternity. Actual infinity in time can never be anything but partial and must therefore be nonabsolute; neither can infinity of actual personality be absolute except in unqualified Deity. And it is the differential of infinity potential in the Unqualified Absolute and the Deity Absolute that eternalizes the Universal Absolute, thereby making it cosmically possible to have material universes in space and spiritually possible to have finite personalities in time.

The concept of infinity is a difficult one for the human mind to grasp, as it is a concept that goes beyond the limits of our physical existence. In this text, the author is making a distinction between two different types of infinity: potential infinity, which is absolute and inseparable from eternity, and actual infinity, which is partial and therefore non-absolute. Potential infinity is inherent in the concept of the Unqualified Absolute and the Deity Absolute, while actual infinity is a concept that can only be partially understood by finite beings in time and space.

The author also suggests that the differential between potential and actual infinity is what eternalizes the Universal Absolute, making it possible for material universes to exist in space and for finite personalities to exist in time. This means that the Universal Absolute serves as a bridge or intermediary between the abstract concepts of potential and actual infinity, allowing them to coexist and interact in the physical universe.

0:11.13 (15.3) The finite can coexist in the cosmos along with the Infinite only because the associative presence of the Universal Absolute so perfectly equalizes the tensions between time and eternity, finity and infinity, reality potential and reality actuality, Paradise and space, man and God. Associatively the Universal Absolute constitutes the identification of the zone of progressing evolional reality existent in the time-space, and in the transcended time-space, universes of subinfinite Deity manifestation.

The concept of the Universal Absolute is related to the idea of the coexistence of finity and infinity, or the material and the spiritual, in the universe. The Universal Absolute is thought to act as a mediator or "associative presence" that allows these seemingly opposing forces to exist together without conflict. It is described as the "adjustment of differential" between these forces, and is believed to be responsible for the eternalization of the cosmos and the possibility of personal growth and evolution within it. The Universal Absolute is also said to be a "positive universe overcontrol in infinity," meaning that it has a pervasive and all-encompassing influence on the universe, but is still subject to the will and purposes of the Paradise Trinity.

0:11.14 (15.4) The Universal Absolute is the potential of the static-dynamic Deity functionally realizable on time-eternity levels as finite-absolute values and as possible of experiential-existential approach. This incomprehensible aspect of Deity may be static, potential, and associative but is not experientially creative or evolutional as concerns the intelligent personalities now functioning in the master universe.

The Universal Absolute is a concept in the cosmic philosophy of The Urantia Book, a text that presents a unique and detailed religious cosmology. The Universal Absolute is described as the resolution of the tension created by the freewill act of the Universal Father, who differentiates universe reality into deified and undeified values. The Universal Absolute is said to be the associative co-ordinator of these sum totals of existential potentialities, and functions as the adjustment of the differential between deity reality and undeified reality inherent in the separation of the dynamics of freewill divinity from the statics of unqualified infinity. It is also said to enable the coexistence of the finite and the Infinite in the cosmos, and to constitute the identification of the zone of progressing evolutional reality in the time-space and transcended time-space universes.

0:11.15 (15.5) *The Absolute.* The two Absolutes—qualified and unqualified—while so apparently divergent in function as they may be observed by mind creatures, are perfectly and divinely unified in and by the Universal Absolute. In the last analysis and in the final comprehension all three are one Absolute. On subinfinite levels they are functionally differentiated, but in infinity they are ONE.

0:11.16 (15.6) We never use the term the Absolute as a negation of aught or as a denial of anything. Neither do we regard the Universal Absolute as self-determinative, a sort of pantheistic and impersonal Deity. The Absolute, in all that pertains to universe personality, is strictly Trinity limited and Deity dominated.

The concept of the Absolute in this text refers to the ultimate reality and truth that encompasses all aspects of the universe. The two Absolutes mentioned, the qualified and unqualified, are different in their function and manifestation, but they are ultimately unified in the Universal Absolute. This ultimate unity of the Absolutes is beyond the understanding of finite beings, but it represents the ultimate truth and reality of the universe. The qualified Absolute is the embodiment of personal Deity, while the unqualified Absolute is the embodiment of non-personal, extradivine, and undeified reality. The Universal Absolute is the synthesis of these two Absolutes, and it represents the resolution of the tension between the finite and the infinite. It is the unifying factor that allows for the coexistence of the finite and the Infinite in the cosmos.

XII. The Trinities

0:12.1 (15.7) The original and eternal Paradise Trinity is existential and was inevitable. This never-beginning Trinity was inherent in the fact of the differentiation of the personal and the nonpersonal by the Father's unfettered will and factualized when his personal will co-ordinated these dual realities by mind. The post-Havona Trinities are experiential—are inherent in the creation of two subabsolute and evolutional levels of power-personality manifestation in the master universe.

The original and eternal Paradise Trinity consists of the three eternal, unchangeable, and perfect beings known as the Universal Father, the Eternal Son, and the Infinite Spirit. These three beings are the source of all existence in the universe, and their relationship is one of perfect unity and harmony.

The post-Havona Trinities, on the other hand, are the result of the evolution of the universe, and they reflect the ongoing process of growth and development that takes place within the universe. These Trinities consist of the Supreme Being, God the Sevenfold, and the Absolute Trinity. The Supreme Being is the result of the unification of the power and personality of the finite beings of the universe, while God the Sevenfold is the result of the unification of the power and personality of the infinite beings of the universe. The Absolute Trinity, on the other hand, is the result of the unification of the power and personality of the absolute beings of the universe.

0:12.2 (15.8) *The Paradise Trinity*—the eternal Deity union of the Universal Father, the Eternal Son, and the Infinite Spirit—is existential in actuality, but all potentials are experiential. Therefore does this Trinity constitute the only Deity reality embracing infinity, and therefore do there occur the universe phenomena of the actualization of God the Supreme, God the Ultimate, and God the Absolute.

The text suggests that the Paradise Trinity, which consists of the Universal Father, the Eternal Son, and the Infinite Spirit, is eternal and exists without beginning or end. However, the potential for other forms of Deity, such as God the Supreme, God the Ultimate, and God the Absolute, are derived from the experiential nature of the universe and its inhabitants. This means that these forms of Deity are not eternal and have a beginning in time and space, but they have the potential to achieve infinite levels of power and personality. The text also suggests that the Trinity is the only form of Deity that fully encompasses infinity, while the other forms are limited by their finite, experiential nature.

0:12.3 (15.9) The first and second experiential Trinities, the post-Havona Trinities, cannot be infinite because they embrace *derived Deities*, Deities evolved by the experiential actualization of realities created or eventuated by the existential Paradise Trinity. Infinity of divinity is being ever enriched, if not enlarged, by finity and absonity of creature and Creator experience.

The first and second experiential Trinities, also known as the post-Havona Trinities, are not infinite in the same way that the eternal Paradise Trinity is infinite. This is because the post-Havona Trinities are comprised of Deities that have evolved or been created by the Paradise Trinity, and therefore are not infinite in the same sense. However, the post-Havona Trinities do contribute to the infinity of divinity by enriching and expanding upon the experiences of creatures and Creators within the universe.

0:12.4 (16.1) Trinities are truths of relationship and facts of co-ordinate Deity manifestation. Trinity functions encompass Deity realities, and Deity realities always seek realization and manifestation in personalization. God the Supreme, God the Ultimate, and even God the Absolute are therefore divine inevitabilities. These three experiential Deities were potential in the existential Trinity, the Paradise Trinity, but their universe emergence as personalities of power is dependent in part on their own experiential functioning in the universes of power and personality and in part on the experiential achievements of the post-Havona Creators and Trinities.

The concept of the Trinity, as discussed in this text, refers to the union of three distinct but inseparable Deity personalities or aspects. The eternal Paradise Trinity is made up of the Universal Father, the Eternal Son, and the Infinite Spirit, and is seen as the source of all existence. The post-Havona Trinities are the result of the evolution and experience of the universe and are seen as potential in the Paradise Trinity. These include God the Supreme, God the Ultimate, and potentially God the Absolute. The idea is that these three experiential Deities are necessary for the realization and manifestation of Deity in the universe.

0:12.5 (16.2) The two post-Havona Trinities, the Ultimate and the Absolute experiential Trinities, are not now fully manifest; they are in process of universe realization. These Deity associations may be described as follows:

0:12.6 (16.3) 1. *The Ultimate Trinity,* now evolving, will eventually consist of the Supreme Being, the Supreme Creator Personalities, and the absonite Architects of the Master Universe, those unique universe planners who are neither creators nor creatures. God the Ultimate will eventually and inevitably powerize and personalize as the Deity consequence of the unification of this experiential Ultimate Trinity in the expanding arena of the well-nigh limitless master universe.

0:12.7   (16.4)   2. *The Absolute Trinity*—the second experiential Trinity—now in process of actualization, will consist of God the Supreme, God the Ultimate, and the unrevealed Consummator of Universe Destiny. This Trinity functions on both personal and superpersonal levels, even to the borders of the nonpersonal, and its unification in universality would experientialize Absolute Deity.

The concept of a Trinity in this context refers to a group of three divine beings or entities who are interconnected and co-exist in a harmonious relationship. In this case, the Paradise Trinity is the original and eternal Trinity, consisting of the Universal Father, the Eternal Son, and the Infinite Spirit. The post-Havona Trinities are the two experiential

Trinities that are currently evolving in the universe, consisting of God the Supreme, God the Ultimate, and possibly God the Absolute. These Trinities are interconnected and work together to manifest and actualize divine power and personality in the universe. The Ultimate and Absolute Trinities are not yet fully manifest and are still in the process of realization.

0:12.8 (16.5) The Ultimate Trinity is experientially unifying in completion, but we truly doubt the possibility of such full unification of the Absolute Trinity. Our concept, however, of the eternal Paradise Trinity is an ever-present reminder that Deity trinitization may accomplish what is otherwise nonattainable; hence do we postulate the sometime appearance of the *Supreme-Ultimate* and the possible trinitization-factualization of God the Absolute.

The text refers to different levels or stages of trinity, which are groupings of three entities that are in some way connected or related. The first is the Paradise Trinity, which is the original and eternal union of the Universal Father, the Eternal Son, and the Infinite Spirit. This trinity is "existential" and was inherent in the nature of the universe from the very beginning.

The second and third trinities mentioned are the Ultimate and Absolute trinities, which are experiential trinities that are currently in the process of realization or actualization. The Ultimate Trinity will eventually consist of the Supreme Being, the Supreme Creator Personalities, and the absonite Architects of the Master Universe. The Absolute Trinity will consist of God the Supreme, God the Ultimate, and the unrevealed Consummator of Universe Destiny.

The text suggests that the Ultimate Trinity will eventually be fully unified, but that the Absolute Trinity may not achieve full unification. However, the concept of the eternal Paradise Trinity serves as a reminder that trinities can achieve great things, and therefore the possibility of the eventual trinitization-factualization of God the Absolute is not ruled out.

0:12.9 (16.6) The philosophers of the universes postulate a *Trinity of Trinities,* an existential-experiential Trinity Infinite, but they are not able to envisage its personalization; possibly it would equivalate to the person of the Universal Father on the conceptual level of the I AM. But irrespective of all this, the original Paradise Trinity is potentially infinite since the Universal Father actually is infinite.

The text suggests that the Paradise Trinity, consisting of the Universal Father, the Eternal Son, and the Infinite Spirit, is potentially infinite due to the fact that the Universal Father is infinite. It also mentions the possibility of a Trinity of Trinities, an existential-experiential Trinity Infinite, which may be equivalent to the person of the Universal Father on the conceptual level of the I AM. However, it is noted that the full personalization of this Trinity is uncertain.

Acknowledgment

0:12.11 (16.8) In formulating the succeeding presentations having to do with the portrayal of the character of the Universal Father and the nature of his Paradise associates, together with an attempted description of the perfect central universe and the encircling seven superuniverses, we are to be guided by the mandate of the superuniverse rulers which directs that we shall, in all our efforts to reveal truth and co-ordinate essential knowledge, give preference to the highest existing human concepts pertaining to the subjects to be presented. We may resort to pure revelation only when the concept of presentation has had no adequate previous expression by the human mind.

0:12.12 (17.1) Successive planetary revelations of divine truth invariably embrace the highest existing concepts of spiritual values as a part of the new and enhanced co-ordination of planetary knowledge. Accordingly, in making these presentations about God and his universe associates, we have selected as the basis of these papers more than one thousand human concepts representing the highest and most advanced planetary knowledge of spiritual values and universe meanings. Wherein these human concepts, assembled from the God-knowing mortals of the past and the present, are inadequate to portray the truth as we are directed to reveal it, we will unhesitatingly supplement them, for this purpose drawing upon our own superior knowledge of the reality and divinity of the Paradise Deities and their transcendent residential universe.

0:12.13 (17.2) We are fully cognizant of the difficulties of our assignment; we recognize the impossibility of fully translating the language of the concepts of divinity and eternity into the symbols of the language of the finite concepts of the mortal mind. But we know that there dwells within the human mind a fragment of God, and that there sojourns with the human soul the Spirit of Truth; and we further know that these spirit forces conspire to enable material man to grasp the reality of spiritual values and to comprehend the philosophy of universe meanings. But even more certainly we know that these spirits of the Divine Presence are able to assist man in the spiritual appropriation of all truth contributory to the enhancement of the ever-progressing reality of personal religious experience—God-consciousness.

0:12.14 (17.3) [Indited by an Orvonton Divine Counselor, Chief of the Corps of Superuniverse Personalities assigned to portray on Urantia the truth concerning the Paradise Deities and the universe of universes.]

Made in the USA
Las Vegas, NV
24 January 2024

84770178R00089